DevOps for Azure Applications

Deploy Web Applications on Azure

Suren Machiraju
Suraj Gaurav

Apress®

DevOps for Azure Applications

Suren Machiraju
Issaquah,
Washington, USA

Suraj Gaurav
Greater Seattle,
Washington, USA

ISBN-13 (pbk): 978-1-4842-3642-0
https://doi.org/10.1007/978-1-4842-3643-7

ISBN-13 (electronic): 978-1-4842-3643-7

Library of Congress Control Number: 2018944115

Managing Director, Apress Media LLC: Welmoed Spahr
Acquisitions Editor: Smriti Srivastava
Development Editor: Matthew Moodie
Coordinating Editor: Divya Modi

Cover designed by eStudioCalamar

Cover image designed by Freepik (www.freepik.com)

Distributed to the book trade worldwide by Springer Science+Business Media New York, 233 Spring Street, 6th Floor, New York, NY 10013. Phone 1-800-SPRINGER, fax (201) 348-4505, e-mail orders-ny@springer-sbm.com, or visit www.springeronline.com. Apress Media, LLC is a California LLC and the sole member (owner) is Springer Science + Business Media Finance Inc (SSBM Finance Inc). SSBM Finance Inc is a **Delaware** corporation.

For information on translations, please e-mail rights@apress.com, or visit http://www.apress.com/rights-permissions.

Apress titles may be purchased in bulk for academic, corporate, or promotional use. eBook versions and licenses are also available for most titles. For more information, reference our Print and eBook Bulk Sales web page at http://www.apress.com/bulk-sales.

Any source code or other supplementary material referenced by the author in this book is available to readers on GitHub via the book's product page, located at www.apress.com/978-1-4842-3642-0. For more detailed information, please visit http://www.apress.com/source-code.

Printed on acid-free paper

With a deep sense of gratitude, I dedicate this book to my brother, Raghu Machiraju, and my sister, Rajasri Kota.

—Surendra Machiraju

I dedicate this book to my mother, Shanti Sinha.

—Suraj Gaurav

Table of Contents

About the Authors

Suren Machiraju developed an innovative supply chain solution that integrated online stores with market makers and aggregators, founding Commercia Corporation in the late 1990s. Within one year, Microsoft acquired Commercia Corp, providing Machiraju with the opportunity to lead the B2B Interoperability team within the BizTalk business unit. Over the next six years, Machiraju's team delivered five releases of the BizTalk Server (2000-2006R2). Subsequently, Machiraju led the BizTalk Rangers, Customer Advisory Group, and in two years, lit up over 20 of the largest middleware deployments on the .NET stack.

In 2011, Machiraju collaborated to create the Azure Customer Advisory Team at Microsoft. For five years, Machiraju led efforts in engaging enterprise customers, startups, and partners for architectural reviews and deployments of cloud/hybrid cloud .NET and OSS applications on the Azure platform. The team pioneered solutions for the most challenging cloud projects and produced dozens of successful deployments.

In 2014, Machiraju accepted appointment as a Technology Business Partner at the Bill & Melinda Gates Foundation, where he collaborates with leading NGOs and non-profit partners in devising technical solutions for some the world's most challenging social issues.

Machiraju holds a Master's Degree in Mechanical Engineering from the Birla Institute of Technology and Science in Pilani, India. He is a listed author of over 20 patents in the business software areas of B2B and Data Interchange Standards and has published books and authored dozens of MSDN articles/technical blogs on Azure and .NET. When he's not publishing blogs or presenting works to the larger technical community, he is enjoying time with his family in the beautiful Pacific Northwest and cheering on the Seahawks each Sunday.

"Please contact me if I can be of assistance in architecting your cloud-based solution; collaborating in this space is one of my greatest passions."

—*Suren* https://about.me/surenmachiraju

Suraj Gaurav started his career in 2000, at the height of dot-com era. He worked at a startup called Asera that was building a revolutionary platform for building B2B applications. In 2002, he moved to Seattle to work for Microsoft. He spent almost 10 years there and worked on various products, including BizTalk server, Commerce platform, and Office 365. He has in-depth experience building enterprise-scale systems like BizTalk, to Internet-scale services like Office 365. He also built the consumption-based billing platform serving as the commerce engine for Azure.

Gaurav holds a Bachelor's degree in Computer Science from Indian Institute of Technology, Kanpur, India. He is listed as an inventor with over 25 patents. When he is not working, he can be found spending time with his family and enjoying the beautiful outdoor life of the Pacific Northwest.

About the Technical Reviewer

Jennifer Curiak specializes in Dynamics 365 implementations, Agile coaching, project management, business analysis, quality assurance, and technical writing. She works to help teams in a variety of industries become more productive, communicate more effectively, and generally get stuff done.

A writer at heart, Curiak started her career as a technical writer for a software company in 2000 and has evolved into designing solutions, managing QA processes and resources, coaching large and small teams in Agile development practices, acting as Scrum Master, and working on Dynamics 365 customizations and implementations. She was the technical reviewer for the books *Administering, Configuring, And Maintaining Microsoft Dynamics 365 in the Cloud* in 2018, and *BizTalk – Azure Applications* in 2018. She continues to write in-house technical and end-user documentation and contributes to other professional publications.

Curiak and her husband Mike live in Western Colorado and spend most of their free time exploring empty and desolate areas of the west by mountain bike and packraft. She can be contacted directly at jcuriak@inotekgroup.com.

Foreword

Listening to the voice of the customer and continuously evolving software is the key to success. The DevOps methodology enables this continuous development; however, the challenge is to navigate the enormous landscape of tools and processes to make it work. This book, DevOps for Azure Deployments, *is the perfect guide to navigate DevOps. Suraj and Suren provide easy-to-read cookbook style instructions on using the tools and ensuring successful deployment of the Azure application.*

I appreciate Suren and Suraj sharing their expertise with the broader community—our business has benefitted from it.

Thank you.

Kevin Bone
CEO
MyCustomerData.com

Introduction

In the world of software development, the need of the hour is short turnaround on all product development lifecycles, also known as the Agile methodology. The Agile methodology is based on customer feedback and supports rapid innovation. Such innovation requires new process and tools. Welcome to DevOps. This book is your hitchhiker's guide to DevOps product development!

Who Should Read This Book?

This is a technical book that provides immense value to developers and release engineers. Project managers will find it useful to understand the workflows related to DevOps.

What You Will Learn

You will learn what it takes to set up a DevOps environment in order to support an Azure deployment. That includes the following topics:

- Overview of DevOps for Azure deployments, including a survey of the available tools.

- Cookbook-style guidance on using the stand-alone tools Octopus Deploy and TeamCity to manage your DevOps environment.

- Cookbook-style guidance on using an integrated developer platform—Microsoft Visual Studio Team Services (VSTS).

- Starter code samples for you to kick-start your environment and processes using the techniques elaborated in the book.

We appreciate your investment in this book. We would love to hear from you to improve this and future offerings.

CHAPTER 1

DevOps for Azure

DevOps is all about automating the application deployment process.
It addresses the drawbacks associated with manual application deployment.
The application deployment process contains several steps—from writing
code to deploying the created release to the target environment, i.e., Microsoft
Azure Cloud. This chapter discusses the need for DevOps, the DevOps
functions, the application deployment process, and the DevOps tools.

The Need for DevOps

Traditionally, the software development lifecycle warranted siloed teams
taking on specific tasks, i.e., the development team and the operations team.
The developers were responsible for writing code, checking in source code
into source control, testing code, QA of code, and staging for deployment.
The Operations/Production team was responsible for deploying the code to
servers and thereafter coordinating with customers and providing feedback
to developers. Such siloed efforts were mostly manual processes with a
small degree of siloed application/software deployment work. This manual
process had several drawbacks, some of which are as follows:

- The communication gap between different teams
  results in resentment and blame, which in turn delays
  fixing errors.

- The entire process took a long time to complete.

© Suren Machiraju, Suraj Gaurav 2018
S. Machiraju and S. Gaurav, *DevOps for Azure Applications*,
https://doi.org/10.1007/978-1-4842-3643-7_1

- The final product did not meet all required criteria.

- Some tools could not be implemented on the production server for security reasons.

- The communication barriers slowed down performance and added to inefficiency.

To cope with these drawbacks, a push for automation arose, leading to the development of DevOps. DevOps is a combination of two terms and two teams—namely Developers and Operations. As the name indicates, it integrates the functionality of both of these teams (Developers and Operations/Production) in the application development and deployment process.

Describing the Functions of DevOps

The basic functions of DevOps are as follows:

- Automates the entire process of application deployment. As a result, the entire process is straightforward and streamlined.

- Allows multiple developers to check in and check out code simultaneously in/from the Source repository.

- Provides a Continuous Integration (CI) server that pools the code from the Source repository and prepares the build by running and passing the unit tests and functional tests automatically.

- Automates testing, integration, deployment, and monitoring tasks.

- Automates workflows and infrastructure.

- Enhances productivity and collaboration through continuous measurement of application performance.

- Allows for rapid and reliable build, test, and release operations of the entire software development process.

DevOps Application Deployment Process

The entire application deployment process is shown in Figure 1-1.

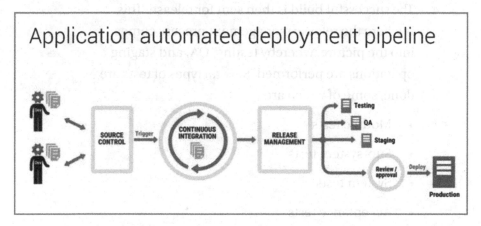

Figure 1-1. *The application deployment process*

Let's now review the various steps in the application deployment process:

1. Developers write code.

2. Code is checked in to the source control/Source repository.

3. Code check-in triggers the Continuous Integration
    (CI) server for generating the build. Automated
    unit testing can be done during the build process.
    Code coverage and code analysis can also be
    performed during this step. If there are build errors,
    unit test failures, or breaches of code coverage
    and code analysis rules, a report is generated
    and automatically sent back to the developer for
    correction.

4. The successful build is then sent for release. This
    is where the release management process comes
    into the picture, whereby testing, QA, and staging
    operations are performed. Several types of tests are
    done, some of which are:

    • Module tests

    • Sub-system tests

    • System tests

    • Acceptance tests

5. In the QA phase, the following types of tests are
    performed:

    • Regression tests

    • Functional tests

    • Performance test

    Once the code passes all of the tests, a release
    version of the software, also called the "golden
    image," is prepared. If any of the preceding tests fail,
    a report about the bug is generated for the team of
    developers who checked in the code.

The development team must first fix the bug and check in the code again. The code goes through the same process of generating the build and release until the code passes all tests.

Figure 1-2 shows the release management process.

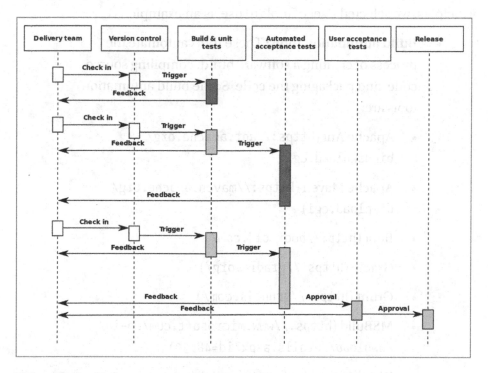

Figure 1-2. *Release management process*

6. The last step in the process is deploying the created release to the target environment—Microsoft Azure Cloud (https://azure.microsoft.com). Once the deployment is complete, all changes in the code are live for users of the target environment in Azure.

Understanding DevOps Tools

There are several DevOps tools available that can help you develop an effective automated environment. You can also use separate tools for performing specific operations in DevOps. A list of tools, based on the broad level functionality, follows. Note that to demonstrate the DevOps principles, we selected a set of tools to use as an example.

- **Build automation tools:** These tools automate the process of creating a software build, compiling source code, and packaging the code. Some build automation tools are:

  - Apache Ant (`https://ant.apache.org/bindownload.cgi`)

  - Apache Maven (`https://maven.apache.org/download.cgi`)

  - Boot (`http://boot-clj.com/`)

  - Gradle (`https://gradle.org/`)

  - Grunt (`https://gruntjs.com/`)

  - MSBuild (`https://www.microsoft.com/en-in/download/details.aspx?id=48159`)

  - Waf (`https://waf.io/`)

- **Continuous Integration tools:** These tools create builds and run tests automatically when the code changes are checked in to the central repository. Some CI tools are:

  - Bamboo (`https://www.atlassian.com/software/bamboo/download`)

  - Buildbot (`https://buildbot.net/`)

- Hudson (http://hudson-ci.org/)

- TeamCity (https://www.jetbrains.com/
  teamcity/download/). *We focus on this tool in this
  book.*

- **Testing tools:** These tools automate the testing process.
  These tools help organizations achieve configuration
  and delivery management needs in a specified time
  frame. Some commonly used testing tools are:

  - Selenium (http://www.seleniumhq.org/)

  - Watir (http://watir.com/)

  - Wapt (https://www.loadtestingtool.com/)

  - Apache JMeter (http://jmeter.apache.org/
    download_jmeter.cgi)

  - QTest (https://www.qasymphony.com/qtest-
    trial-qascom/)

- **Version control system:** This is a configuration
  management system that takes care of all the changes
  made to documents, codes, files, etc. Some commonly
  used version control systems are:

  - Subversion (https://subversion.apache.org/)

  - Team Foundation Server (TFS) (https://www.
    visualstudio.com/tfs/). We focus on this tool in
    this book.

  - GIT (https://git-scm.com/)

  - Mercurial (https://www.mercurial-scm.org/)

  - Perforce (https://www.perforce.com/)

- **Code review tools:** These tools help organizations improve the quality of their code. Some code review tools are:

  - Crucible (`https://www.atlassian.com/software/crucible`)

  - Gerrit (`https://www.gerritcodereview.com/`)

  - GitHub (`https://github.com/`)

  - Bitbucket Server (`https://www.atlassian.com/software/bitbucket/server`)

- **Continuous Delivery/release management tools:** These tools automate the process of building and testing code changes for release to production. Some of these tools are:

  - XL Release (`https://xebialabs.com/products/xl-release/`)

  - ElectricFlow (`http://electric-cloud.com/products/electricflow/`)

  - Serena Release (`https://www.microfocus.com/serena/`)

  - Octopus Deploy (`https://octopus.com/downloads`). *We focus on this tool in this book.*

- **All-in-one platforms:** These tools combine the functionalities of previously listed tools. Some all-in-one platforms are:

  - ProductionMap (`http://www.productionmap.com/`)

  - Jenkins (`https://jenkins.io/`)

- Microsoft Visual Studio Team Services (VSTS) (`https://www.visualstudio.com/team-services/`). *We focus on this tool in this book.*

- AWS CodePipeline (`https://aws.amazon.com/codepipeline/getting-started/`)

With a basic understanding of the fundamentals, you're ready to move forward and dive deeper into the specifics. We start by discussing stand-alone tools, and thereafter discuss an all-in-one integrated platform.

Summary

This chapter discussed the importance of DevOps over the manual process of application deployment. DevOps integrates the functionality of both teams (Developers and Operations/Production) in the application development and deployment process. This chapter provided information about the basic functions of DevOps. The entire process of application deployment was discussed. Toward the end of the chapter, a list of DevOps tools was provided.

CHAPTER 2

Deployment via TeamCity and Octopus Deploy

As discussed in the previous chapter, application deployment in DevOps requires a Continuous Integration (CI) tool and Continuous Delivery (CD) tool/release management software to automate the entire process. Currently, there are several tools available in the market. This chapter discusses three best-of-breed tools—TeamCity as a CI tool, Octopus Deploy as a release management tool, and CD software to deploy the package on the Azure web application. Since different vendors deliver these best-of-breed tools, there is some complexity involved in integrating them into a single solution.

Introduction to Microsoft Public Cloud, Azure

Before we delve into the DevOps tools, let's recap the deployment environment. As a reminder, we are focusing on Microsoft Azure. However, be assured that information from this chapter can be applied to other public cloud solutions.

© Suren Machiraju, Suraj Gaurav 2018
S. Machiraju and S. Gaurav, *DevOps for Azure Applications*,
https://doi.org/10.1007/978-1-4842-3643-7_2

Azure has the capability to host applications. These applications can be further integrated with other applications and services on the Azure platform rather easily. Azure's integration features provide customers with enhanced business agility and efficiency. They help users deploy the source code to multiple Azure websites.

Understanding TeamCity

TeamCity is a CI server for developers and is powered by JetBrains. It provides several relevant features:

- Supports different platforms/tools/languages
- Automates the build and deployment processes
- Enhances quality and standards across teams
- Works as an artifact and NuGet repository
- Provides a reporting and statistics feature

Definition   According to Martin Fowler, "Continuous Integration is a software development practice in which developers commit code changes into a shared repository several times a day. Each commit is followed by an automated build to ensure that new changes integrate well into the existing code base and to detect problems early."

Basic Concepts of TeamCity

Here are the basic concepts of TeamCity:

- **Project:** Refers to a set of build configurations.
- **Build configuration:** Refers to a collection of settings (VCS roots, build steps, and build triggers) that define a build procedure.

- **VCS root:** Refers to a set of version control settings (source path, username, password, etc.) that allow TeamCity to interact with a version control system for managing the modifications and sources for a build.

- **Build step:** Refers to a task to be executed by the server. It is represented by a build runner.

- **Build runner:** Integrates different tools, including the build tool (Ant, Gradle, MSBuild, PowerShell, etc.), a testing framework (JUnit, NUnit, etc.), and a code analysis engine. It describes the build workflow.

- **Build agent:** Refers to an application that is responsible for executing the build process. It helps developers get faster feedback, as different tests can be run simultaneously on different platforms supported by the build agent.

- **TeamCity server:** Refers to the server application, which manages all build agents, manages the sequence of builds to build agents, and conveys the results.

- **Build:** Refers to the program/application version.

- **Build trigger:** Refers to a rule that automatically starts a new build when a specified event occurs.

- **Build queue:** Refers to a sequence of builds that are triggered and not yet started. These builds are assigned to the respective agents when they are available.

- **Build artifact:** Refers to the set of files (installers, WAR files, reports, log files, etc.) generated by the build process.

Configuring a Build in TeamCity

In this section, we configure arguments for the PowerShell script in TeamCity. This will enable TeamCity to execute the PowerShell script. For this scenario, we created a PowerShell script named `[string]App.Ps1`.

The build configuration uses a step-oriented approach, which is outlined in the following sections.

Step 1: Creating a Project

To configure a build in TeamCity, first create a project. There are several options available for this task, as follows:

- Manually

- Pointing to a repository URL

- Pointing to a GitHub.com repository

- Pointing to a Bitbucket Cloud repository

Perform the following steps to create a standard project:

1. Click the Administration link in the top-right corner of the Administration area.

2. Click the down arrow button beside the Create Project button. A drop-down list appears.

3. Select the Manually option from the drop-down list to create a project manually. After you click the Manual option, the Create New Project page appears.

4. Enter the desired name of the project in the Name text box.

5. Enter the desired ID of the project in the Project ID text box.

6. Enter the desired description of the project in the Description text box.

7. Click the Create button to create the project.

Now, the project has been created.

Step 2: Creating a Build Configuration

Build configurations describe the process by which a project's sources are fetched and built. Once the project is created, TeamCity prompts you to create build configurations. Alternatives to create build configurations are as follows:

- Manually

- Pointing to a repository URL

- Pointing to a GitHub.com repository

- Pointing to a Bitbucket Cloud repository

Perform the following steps to create a build configuration manually:

1. Click the down arrow button beside the Create Build Configuration button. A drop-down list appears.

2. Select the Manual option from the drop-down list to create the build configuration manually.

3. Specify the name of the build configuration in the Name text box.

4. Specify the build configuration ID in the Build Configuration ID text box.

5. Specify the desired description in the Description text box.

6. Click the Save button. Figure 2-1 shows the General Settings page.

Figure 2-1. *General Settings page*

Step 3: Configuring the Version Control Settings

In this step, we provide settings related to the VCS root. The VCS root
describes a connection to a version control system, and there are several
settings associated with it. These settings allow VCS to communicate with
TeamCity. They define the way changes are monitored and sources are
specified for a build. Perform the following steps to configure the version
control settings:

1. Select the Version Control Settings tab.

2. Click the Attach VCS Root button. The New VCS
   Root page appears.

3. Select the desired type of VCS from the Type of VCS
   drop-down list. We selected Subversion.

4. Specify a unique VCS root name in the VCS Root
   Name text box.

5. Specify a unique VCS root ID in the VCS Root ID
   text box.

The connection settings appear on the page depending on the type of VCS selected. In our case, the SVN Connection Settings section appears.

6. Specify the repository URL in the URL text box.

7. To allow TeamCity to communicate with the Source repository, specify the username and password in the Username and Password text boxes, respectively.

8. Click the Test Connection button to test the connection. This validates that TeamCity can communicate with the repository. A Test Connection message box appears with the Connection Successful message. If the connection shows failure, check the specified URL and the credentials.

9. Click the Create button. Figure 2-2 shows the settings for the New VCS Root page.

Figure 2-2. *Settings for the New VCS Root page*

Step 4: Configuring the Build Steps

Once the VCS root is created, we can configure the build steps. Perform the following steps to add a build step:

1. Select the Build Steps tab.

2. Click the Add Build Step button. The Build Step page appears.

3. Select the PowerShell option from the Runner Type drop-down list.

Note   In this example, we use the PowerShell script file named [string]App.ps1. This file compiles the source code.

---

4. Specify the desired step name in the Step Name text box.

5. Select the desired step execution policy from the Execute Step drop-down list.

6. Select the File option from the Script drop-down list.

7. Specify the path to the PowerShell script in the Script File box. This field contains the physical path mapped to the [string]App.ps1 script, which is located on the build agent, as shown in Figure 2-3.

Figure 2-3. *Creating a build step*

8. Specify the PowerShell script execution mode in the Script Execution Mode option.

9. Enter script arguments in the Script Arguments section. We entered five arguments that will be passed to the [string]App.ps1 script during execution by TeamCity.

ARGUMENTS PASSED TO THE POWERSHELL SCRIPT

All arguments should be explained in terms of their relative paths. Descriptions of all the arguments passed to the PowerShell script follow:

- ..\Workflow: Allows the PowerShell script to access the contents of the Workflow folder.

- ..\Central: Allows the PowerShell script to access the contents of the Central folder.

- ..\Server: Allows the PowerShell script to access the contents of the Server folder.

- `Nuget.exe`: Allows the PowerShell script to load the `Nuget.exe` file, which is located on the build agent.

- `v. Targetfolder`: Specifies the path of a folder on the build agent where the compiled code is placed.

10.   Click the Save button, as shown in Figure 2-4.

Figure 2-4. *Saving the build step*

A successful build is created in TeamCity, which is executable through the PowerShell script [string]App.ps1, as shown in Figure 2-5.

Figure 2-5. *Successful build message*

Creating a Package

Once TeamCity creates a successful build, changes may need to be made
to the PowerShell script ([string]App.ps1). For example, we may need
to make changes to NugetExePath to accept a new argument, as shown in
Figure 2-6.

```
Param(
    [String]$WorkflowFolder,
    [String]$CentralFolder,
    [String]$ServerFolder,
    [String]$NugetExePath,
    [String]$TargetFolder
    # [switch]$overwrite
)


function ZipFiles( $zipfilename, $sourcedir )
{
    Add-Type -Assembly System.IO.Compression.FileSystem
    $compressionLevel = [System.IO.Compression.CompressionLevel]::Optimal
    [System.IO.Compression.ZipFile]::CreateFromDirectory($sourcedir,
        $zipfilename, $compressionLevel, $false)
}

$WorkflowFolder = Resolve-Path $WorkflowFolder
$CentralFolder = Resolve-Path $CentralFolder
$ServerFolder = Resolve-Path $ServerFolder



Write-Host "Processing zipping of files" $TargetFolder
$BuildFileName =  Join-Path "C:\Temp_SAPP" 'Build.zip'

ZipFiles $BuildFileName "C:\Temp_SAPP"

Copy-Item  $BuildFileName $TargetFolder -force

if($NugetExePath -ne "")
{

Set-Location $TargetPublishPath
$arg1="spec"
$arg2="pack"

&$NugetExePath $arg1
&$NugetExePath $arg2

}

Write-Host "Processing completed and files placed at: "  $TargetFolder
```

Figure 2-6. *Making changes to NugetExePath*

The changes made to the PowerShell script create a package in the target folder.

Figure 2-7 shows the created NuGet package.

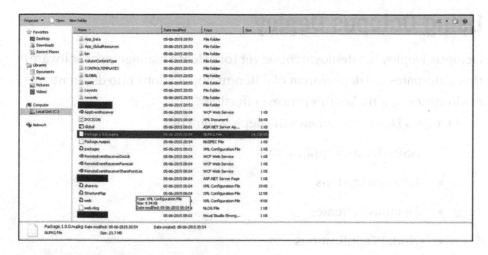

Figure 2-7. *The NuGet package*

Copy this NuGet package from the build agent to where it will be imported into the Octopus server for deployment purposes, as shown in Figure 2-8.

Figure 2-8. *NuGet package ready for deployment*

Using Octopus Deploy

Octopus Deploy is a deployment server (or release management software) that automates the deployment of different applications into different environments. It makes this process effortless.

Octopus Deploy automates the deployment of:

- ASP.NET web applications
- Java applications
- Database updates
- NodeJS applications
- Custom scripts

Octopus Deploy supports the following environments:

- Development
- Test
- Production

Octopus Deploy provides a consistent deployment process to support the deployment needs of team members; an Octopus user can define a process for deploying the software. The Octopus user can specify different environments for different applications and can set privileges for different team members to deploy to different environments. For example, a team member can be authorized to deploy to a test environment while also being restricted to the production deployment.

Note   The latest MSI of Octopus Deploy can be downloaded at `https://octopus.com/downloads`.

Creating a Project

Octopus Deploy allows users to create projects. In Octopus Deploy, a project is a set of deliverable components, including websites and database scripts. A project is created within Octopus Deploy to manage multiple software projects across different environments. For instance, if there are six developers working on the same business project, we need to create a single project in Octopus Deploy.

Perform the following steps to create a project:

1. Navigate to the Projects area.

2. Click the Add Project button. The Create Project page opens.

3. Specify a relevant name for the project in the Name text box.

4. Specify a relevant description for the project in the Description text area.

5. Select the desired option from the Project Group drop-down list.

6. Select the desired lifecycle from the Lifecycle drop-down list.

7. Click the Save button, as shown in Figure 2-9.

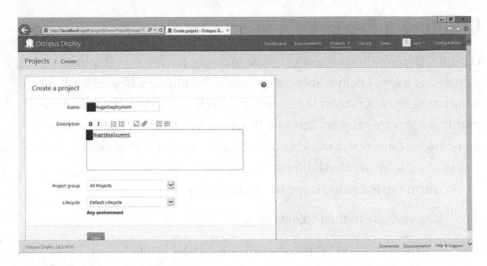

Figure 2-9. *Steps to create a project*

Note   A lifecycle is used to replicate deployments between
environments automatically.

Creating an Environment

An environment is a group of machines to which the software is deployed
simultaneously. Common environments in the Octopus Deploy are Test,
Acceptance, Staging, and Production. In other words, an environment
can be defined as a group of deployment targets (Windows servers,
Linux servers, Microsoft Azure, etc.). For the current scenario, we are
creating two environments so that we can deploy to two websites. Each
environment represents a single tenant.

Perform the following steps to create an environment:

1. Navigate to the Environments area.

2. Click the Add Environment button to add an environment. The Environment Settings page opens.

3. Enter a relevant name for the environment in the Name text box. In this case, we entered Test1.

4. Enter a relevant description of the environment in the Description text box.

5. Click the Save button, as shown in Figure 2-10.

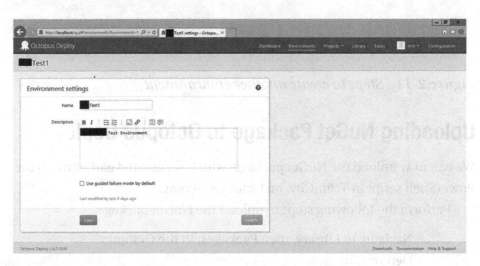

Figure 2-10. *Steps to create an environment*

Similarly, create another environment with the name Test2, as shown in Figure 2-11.

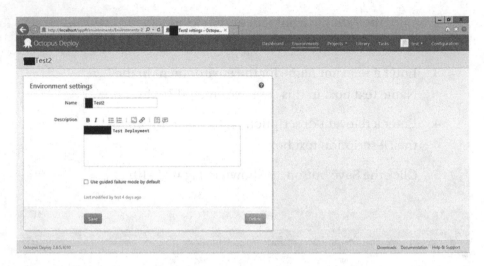

Figure 2-11. *Steps to create another environment*

Uploading NuGet Package to Octopus Deploy

We can now upload the NuGet package, which we created earlier using the PowerShell script in TeamCity, on Octopus Deploy.

Perform the following steps to upload the NuGet package:

1. Navigate to Library, then Packages, in the Octopus Deploy interface.

2. Click the Upload Package button, as shown in Figure 2-12.

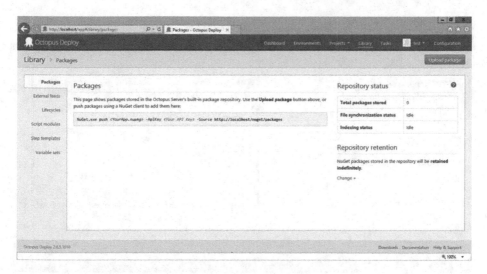

Figure 2-12. *Clicking the Upload Package button*

The Upload a NuGet Package page appears.

3. Click the Browse button beside the NUPKG File option. The Choose File to Upload dialog box appears.

4. Navigate to the package's location. As discussed earlier, we copied the package to the Package Source folder.

5. Select the package.

6. Click the Open button, as shown in Figure 2-13.

29

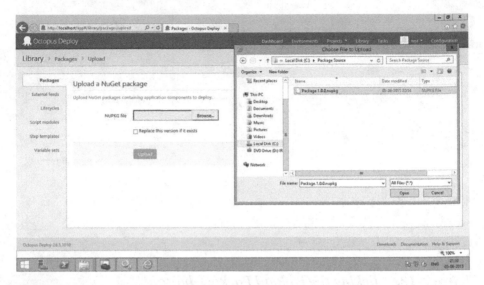

Figure 2-13. *Uploading a NuGet package*

The name of the selected package file with its complete path appears in the NUPKG File box.

7. Click the Upload button.

After clicking the Upload button, the package file starts uploading.

Creating Steps for the Deployment Process

As discussed earlier, Octopus Deploy allows users to define the deployment process for their project easily. Users can add steps to the deployment process using templates, including built-in step templates, custom step templates, and community contributed step templates.

Users can also select the Add Step button to display a list of templates and then select the desired step. The built-in steps can be used to handle common deployment scenarios.

In the current scenario, we created the following two steps for the deployment process:

- **NugetDeploy:** This step deploys a NuGet package to one or more machines, which are running the Tentacle deployment agent.

- **Web Deploy-Publish Website (MSDeploy):** This step is created to deploy the NuGet package to Azure websites by running a PowerShell script across machines.

Perform the following steps to add the NugetDeploy step:

1. Select the Process tab.

2. Click the Add Step button. The Choose Step Type pop-up appears with a list of built-in step templates.

3. Select the desired built-in step template. In this case, we selected the Deploy a NuGet Package option. The Step Details page appears.

4. Enter a name for step in the Step Name text box. In this case, we entered NugetDeploy.

5. Specify the target machines in the Machine Roles text box. In this case, we selected WebRole.

6. Select the desired package feed from the NuGet Feed drop-down list.

7. Click the Add button. Figure 2-14 shows the details of the NugetDeploy step.

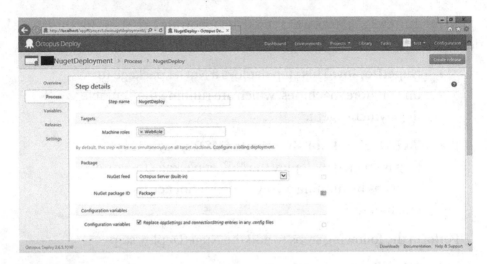

Figure 2-14. *The NugetDeploy step*

In Figure 2-14, we see that the NuGet Package ID field contains the name of the NuGet package that was uploaded earlier.

Similarly, we can add a step using the custom step template with the name Web Deploy-Publish Website (MSDeploy), as shown in Figure 2-15.

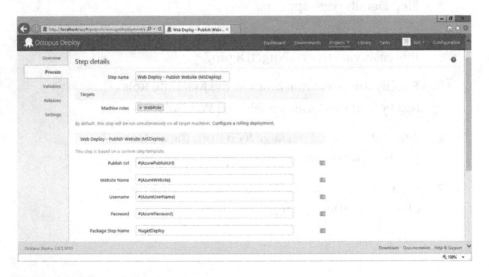

Figure 2-15. *Adding a step*

We can look at the created steps by selecting the Process tab of the created project, as shown in Figure 2-16.

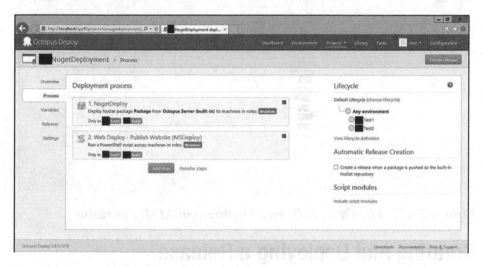

Figure 2-16. *Displaying the created steps*

Using Variables

Variables are required for eliminating the need for hard-coding the configuration values to support different environments easily. They are required while deploying packages to Azure websites. As a NuGet package is shared between two sites, we used the OctopusBypassDeploymentMutex variable to avoid resource locking of the NuGet package, as shown in Figure 2-17.

Figure 2-17. *The OctopusBypassDeploymentMutex variable*

Creating and Deploying a Release

A release contains all details of the project and package so that it can be deployed to different environments as per requirements. Perform the following steps to create a release:

1. Navigate to the Overview page, which displays all details of the project.

2. Click the Create Release button. The Create page appears.

3. Enter the desired release version in the Version text box.

4. Select the desired package from the Package column.

5. Enter the desired release notes in the Release Notes text area.

6. Click the Save button. Figure 2-18 shows the process of creating a release.

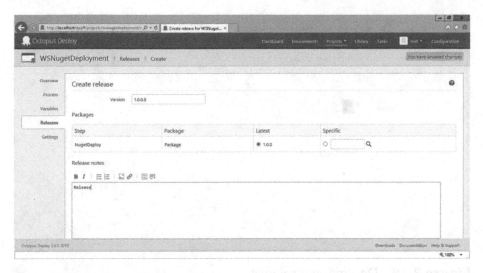

Figure 2-18. *Creating a release*

Note   In the current scenario, we are creating a release to deploy the NuGet package to multiple Azure websites.

A release is created with the specified version. The Deploy page opens. Here, we can select the desired environment to which we want to deploy the created release. We can also click the Change button to change the environment.

7. Click the Deploy Now button to deploy the created release, as shown in Figure 2-19.

Figure 2-19. *Deploying a release*

The release is deployed successfully to both Azure websites, as shown
in Figure 2-20.

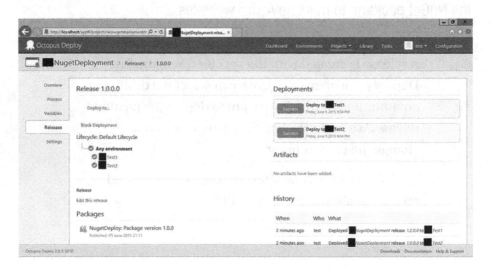

Figure 2-20. *Deployment result*

We can now navigate to the Azure portal where we see that two Azure websites have been created for multiple deployments of the NuGet package, as shown in Figure 2-21.

Figure 2-21. *Displaying the created websites on Azure*

Summary

In this chapter, we discussed the CI tool called TeamCity and the release management software or CD tool called Octopus Deploy. TeamCity builds the source code using MSBuild. Initially, we configured TeamCity by creating a new project and providing the SVN path to fetch the latest code onto the build agent. We then configured the source code and set parameters for the PowerShell script file. The target path settings were modified to create a NuGet package. This package was copied from the build agent to a location where Octopus Deploy could pick it up.

In Octopus Deploy, we created a project and two environments to test multiple deployment scenarios. Then, we uploaded the package. We also created two steps—NugetDeploy and Web Deploy-Publish Website (MSDeploy). The former was created to deploy the uploaded NuGet package onto a Tentacle machine while the latter was created to deploy the contents of the NuGet package from the Tentacle machine to the Azure websites.

We also configured variables and credentials for both environments. Lastly, we created a release for the project, which could be deployed to different environments. The release allowed us to deploy the contents of NuGet package onto Azure websites in parallel. In the end, we executed the release and found that the content of the NuGet package was deployed successfully.

CHAPTER 3

Deployment via VSTS

In the last chapter, we discussed the process of deploying applications to Azure using best-of-breed and stand-alone DevOps tools: TeamCity as a CI tool, and Octopus Deploy as a CD tool. The challenge with the example solution is that there are separate tools used to deploy applications. In this chapter, we review a DevOps platform, an all-encompassing end-to-end solution called Microsoft Visual Studio Team Services (VSTS); see www.visualstudio.com/team-services/.

VSTS is a collaborative solution that takes care of the entire software deployment lifecycle, from creating packages to deploying the application. One of its major strengths is its tight integration with Azure. This chapter steps through the entire process of application deployment to Azure using VSTS.

Understanding VSTS

Visual Studio Team Services (VSTS) is an Application Lifecycle Management (ALM) system that manages the entire process of the software development lifecycle. In earlier versions, it was known as Visual Studio Online (VSO).

© Suren Machiraju, Suraj Gaurav 2018
S. Machiraju and S. Gaurav, *DevOps for Azure Applications*,
https://doi.org/10.1007/978-1-4842-3643-7_3

Features of VSTS

Some of the features of VSTS are as follows:

- Provides integrated software development.

- Supports source control systems, including Git and Team Foundation Version Control (TFVC).

- Supports several features that can be used to track product features, bugs, and other issues.

- Supports several Agile methods for planning purposes.

- Automates the build, test, and release processes for rapid release of the software.

- Supports usage across massively scaled-out teams consisting of thousands of members.

- Provides a reliable and scalable service that is available 24 hours a day, seven days a week, and is backed by a 99.9% Service License Agreement (SLA).

- Allows users to customize elements such as source control, work tracking, build and release, and test, etc., according to business requirements.

- Allows users to add more functionality to Visual Studio Marketplace, service hooks, REST APIs, and Visual Studio SDKs.

Advantages of VSTS

VSTS is a Microsoft product introduced to upgrade Team Foundation Server (TFS). Therefore, it is also known as a cloud version of TFS. Some of the advantages of VSTS are as follows:

- Free for up to five users.

- Operations and maintenance costs are lower than TFS, as it is a cloud-based solution, while TFS is an on-premise solution.

- Encourages more stakeholders to get involved as they can log on to the platform from anywhere and at any time.

- Allows developers to write and commit code from anywhere.

- Enables effortless inter-team communication, as it supports the Git source control system, which provides the cross-platform facility.

- Ideal platform for organizations to develop a modern DevOps environment.

Creating an Account in VSTS

One of the primary tasks while using VSTS is creating an account to host the project. Perform the following steps to create an account in VSTS:

1. Navigate to the link `https://www.visualstudio.com/team-services/`.

2. Click the Get Started for Free button, as shown in Figure 3-1.

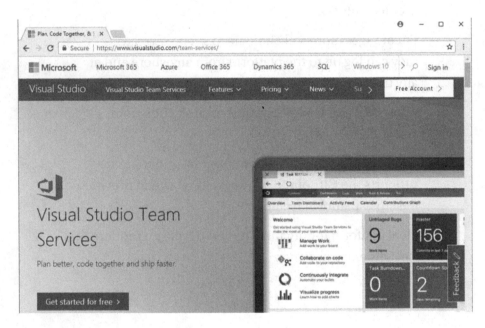

Figure 3-1. *Launching Visual Studio Team Services*

The Sign Into Your Account page appears.

3. Enter the desired Microsoft email address in the Email or Phone text box.

4. Click the Next button, as shown in Figure 3-2.

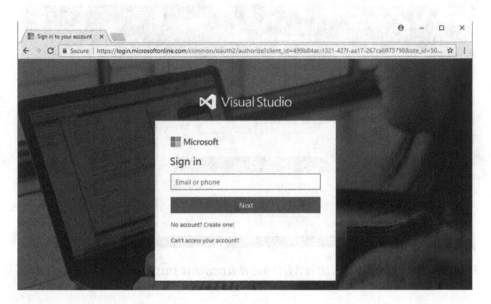

Figure 3-2. *Sign in page – user name*

Note   You can use your Microsoft credentials to sign in to Visual Studio Team Services.

---

5. Enter the required password in the Password field.

6. Click the Sign In button, as shown in Figure 3-3.

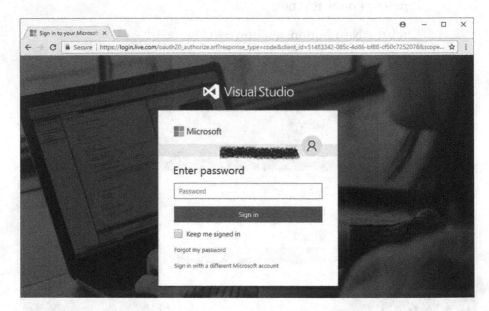

Figure 3-3. *Sign in with a Microsoft account password*

The Account Creation page appears.

7. Enter the desired name of the account in the text box beside the Host My Projects At The label. This enables you to specify a host location (US, India, etc.) for the projects.

8. Select the desired radio button below the Manage Code Using The option. This specifies the repository for Git to manage the code.

9. Click the Continue button, as shown in Figure 3-4.

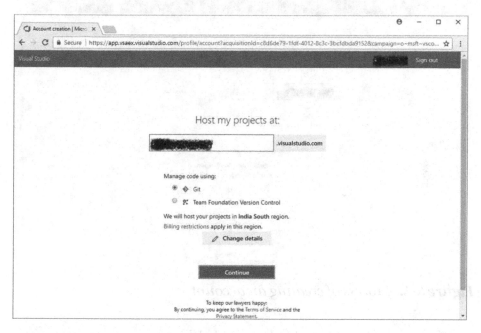

Figure 3-4. *Account for hosting project*

After you click the Continue button, the process of creating an account begins, as shown in Figure 3-5.

Figure 3-5. *Process of creating an account*

The account is created with the specified name.

Creating a Project

After we create an account in VSTS, the first page, Create New Project, asks users to create a new project. Perform the following steps to create a project:

1. Enter the desired name for the project in the Project Name text box.

2. Enter the desired description for the project in the Description text area.

3. Select the desired version control from the Version
    Control drop-down list. In this case, we selected Git.

4. Select the desired work item process from the
    Work Item Process drop-down list. In this case, we
    selected Agile.

5. Click the Create button to create the project, as
    shown in Figure 3-6.

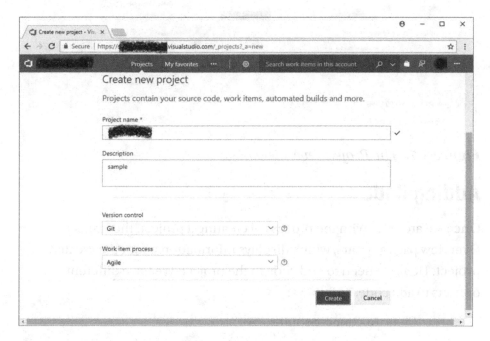

Figure 3-6. *Steps to create a project*

The project is created with the specific settings and opens with the
Project Overview page, as shown in Figure 3-7.

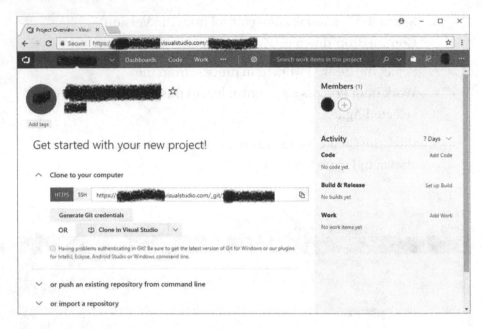

Figure 3-7. *The Project Overview page*

Adding Code

Once we are done with the process of creating a project, the Project Overview page appears, which displays information about the created project. Here, we need to add code to the project. We have different options to add code, as follows:

- Clone to your computer

- Push an existing repository from the command line

- Import a repository

Perform the following steps to add code to the project:

1. Select the Code tab.

2. Click the Clone in Visual Studio button, as shown in Figure 3-8.

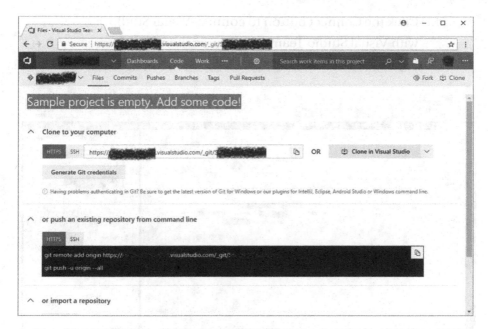

Figure 3-8. *Adding code in Visual Studio*

A message box appears requesting confirmation.

3. Click the Open Microsoft Visua...ndler Selector button to open Visual Studio, as shown in Figure 3-9.

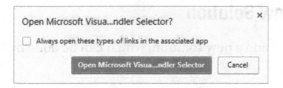

Figure 3-9. *Launching Microsoft Visual Studio Selector*

The Microsoft Visual Studio window opens with the Visual Studio Team Services dialog box. In this dialog box, we see the remote and local paths.

4. Click the Connect button to connect Visual Studio
with Visual Studio Team Services, as shown in
Figure 3-10.

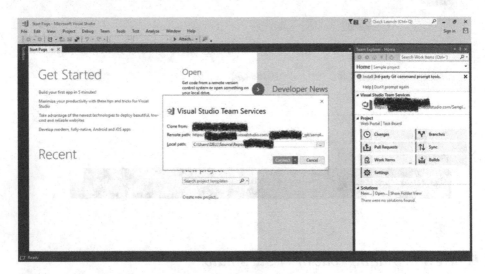

Figure 3-10. *Connecting Visual Studio to Visual Studio Team
Services*

After we click Connect, the cloning and connection processes are
complete.

Adding a New Solution

Here, we need to add a new solution, which can be done by performing the
following steps:

1. Click the New link under the Solutions section in
the Team Explorer panel. The New Project window
appears.

2. Select the desired option from the left pane. In this
case, we selected Web. The related templates appear
in the middle pane based on the selection.

3. Select the desired template in the middle pane. In this case, we selected ASP.NET Web Application (.NET Framework).

4. Enter the desired name for the selected template in the Name text box. In this case, we entered WebApp.

5. Specify the desired location for the template in the Location text box.

6. Select the Create Directory for Solution checkbox.

7. Select the Create New Git Repository checkbox.

8. Click the OK button, as shown in Figure 3-11.

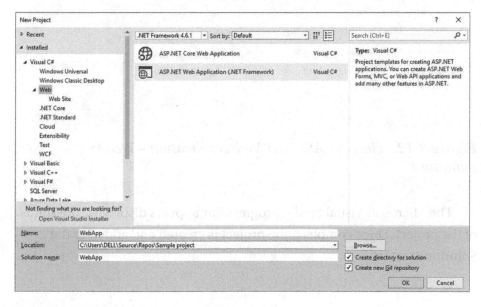

Figure 3-11. *Creating a new project*

The New ASP.NET Web Application – WebApp window appears.

9. Select the MVC option to create the MVC application.

10. Click the OK button, as shown in Figure 3-12.

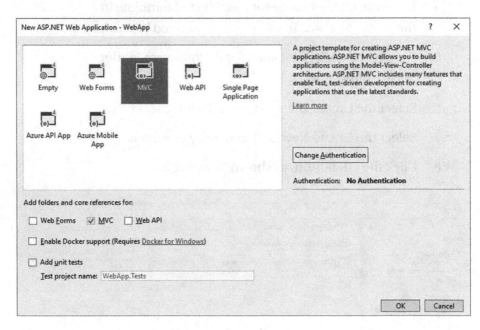

Figure 3-12. *The New ASP.NET Web Application – WebApp window*

The Microsoft Visual Studio progress bar appears displaying the status of the project. Once complete, the project is created and added to the Solutions section.

Committing Changes

Once the required changes are made, we can commit them. Perform the following steps to commit the changes:

1. Click the Changes button under the Project section in the Team Explorer panel, as shown in Figure 3-13.

Figure 3-13. *Steps to commit changes*

The changes made to the project are displayed in the Changes section.

2. Enter the desired commit message in the Enter a Commit Message text box.

3. Click the Commit All button, as shown in Figure 3-14.

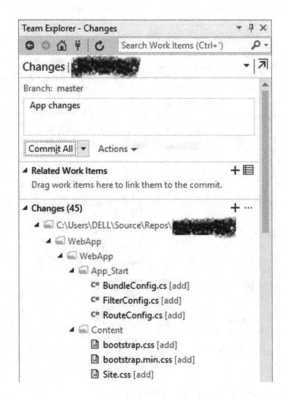

Figure 3-14. *Steps to commit changes*

A commit is created locally.

4.   Click the Sync link to share the changes with the
server, as shown in Figure 3-15.

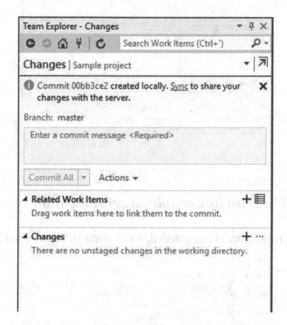

Figure 3-15. *Sharing the changes with the server*

The Synchronization page appears in the Team
Explorer panel.

5.   Click the Push link under the Outgoing Commits
section, as shown in Figure 3-16.

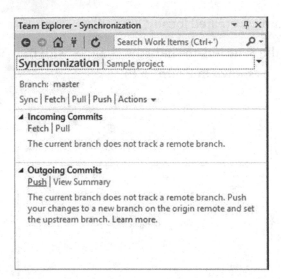

Figure 3-16. *The Push link enables synchronization*

The synchronization is successful, as shown in Figure 3-17.

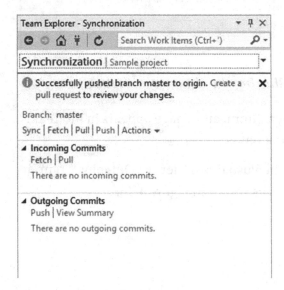

Figure 3-17. *Successful synchronization*

At this point, the code is added to the server.

Next, verify the repository in VSTS. For this, navigate to the Code section of the project created earlier. A folder with the same name as that of the project created in Visual Studio appears, as shown in Figure 3-18.

Figure 3-18. *The repository*

Creating a Build

Once the source control repository is available, we can set up (or create) a build. Perform the following steps to create a build:

1. Hover the mouse over the Build and Release tab. A list of options appears.

2. Click the Builds option, as shown in Figure 3-19.

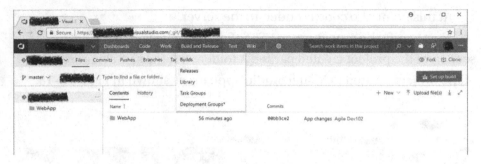

Figure 3-19. *The Builds option*

The My Definitions page appears.

3. Click the New button to create a new build
definition, as shown in Figure 3-20.

Figure 3-20. *Creating a new build definition*

The Select Build Definition Template page appears.

4. Select the desired template from the Select a
Template list.

5. Click the Apply button, as shown in Figure 3-21.

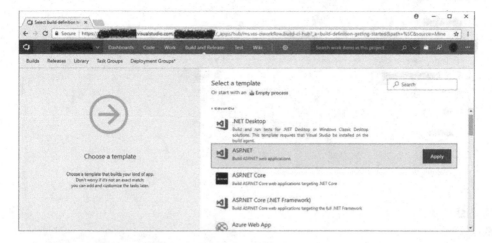

Figure 3-21. *Selecting a template*

The Sample Project-ASP.NET page appears.

6. Enter the desired name for the template in the Name text box.

7. Select the desired option from the Azure Queue drop-down list.

8. Specify the desired parameters under the Parameters section.

9. Click the Save & Queue button. A drop-down list appears.

10. Select the Save option from the drop-down list, as shown in Figure 3-22.

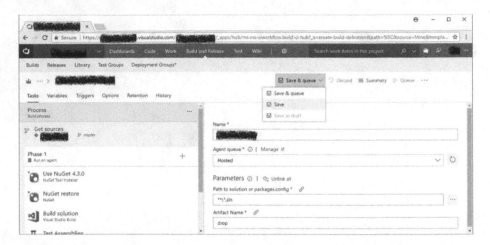

Figure 3-22. *Tasks tab of the Sample Project-ASP.NET page*

> The Save Build Definition dialog box appears.

11. Select the desired folder in which to save the build definition. In this case, we selected the parent folder.

12. Enter the desired comment in the Comment text area.

13. Click the Save button to save the build definition, as shown in Figure 3-23.

Figure 3-23. *The Save Build Definition dialog box*

14. Select the Variables tab to view the associated variables, as shown in Figure 3-24.

Figure 3-24. *The Variables tab*

15. Select the Triggers tab to set the triggers. The related options appear in the right pane.

16. Select the Enable Continuous Integration checkbox to enable continuous integration.

17. Select the Batch Changes While a Build Is in Progress checkbox to accept the batch changes during the build.

18. Specify branch filters under the Branch Filters section, as shown in Figure 3-25.

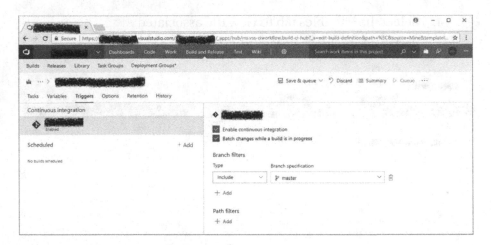

Figure 3-25. *Setting triggers*

19.   Select the Options tab. The related settings appear.

20.   Specify the desired general build definition setting under the Build Properties section.

21.   Specify the desired build job authorization and timeout settings under the Build Job section.

22.   Click the Save & Queue button. A drop-down list appears.

23.   Select the Save & Queue option to save and queue the settings, as shown in Figure 3-26.

Figure 3-26. *Save and queue the build*

The Save Build Definition and Queue dialog box appear.

24. View the settings and make the changes as per the requirements, as shown in Figure 3-27.

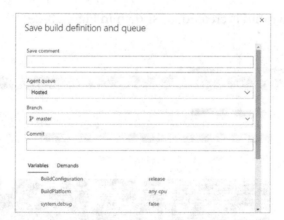

Figure 3-27. *The Save Build Definition and Queue dialog box*

25.   Click the Save button to create a build.

A build with a build number is queued.

26.   Click the build number, as shown in Figure 3-28.

Figure 3-28. *Clicking the build number*

A successful build is created, as shown in Figure 3-29.

Figure 3-29. *Creation of a successful build*

View the build summary by clicking the build number, as shown in Figure 3-30.

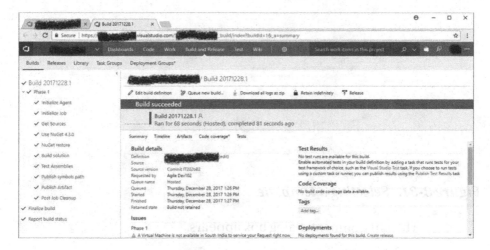

Figure 3-30. *Build summary*

Creating a Release Definition

A release definition describes an application's end-to-end release process so that it can be deployed to different environments. Perform the following steps to create a release definition:

1. Select the Releases tab.

2. Click the New Definition button. The Select a Template dialog box appears.

3. Select the desired template for the release from the Select a Template dialog box.

4. Click the Apply button, as shown in Figure 3-31.

Figure 3-31. Selecting a template

The Environment dialog box appears.

5. Type the desired name for the environment in the Environment Name text box.

6. Click the Close icon in the Environment dialog box to close it.

7. Select the Tasks tab. A drop-down list appears.

8. Select the environment that was created earlier.

9. Select the Azure subscription from the Azure Subscription drop-down list.

Note   We need to have a resource group on Azure to deploy our application.

---

10. Select the type of app from the App Type drop-down list.

11. Select the app service name from the App Service Name drop-down list.

12. Click the Save button to save all the settings, as shown in Figure 3-32.

Figure 3-32. *Setting the task's properties*

The Save dialog box appears.

13. Select the desired folder from the Folder drop-down list.

14. Specify the desired comment in the Comment text box.

15. Click the OK button, as shown in Figure 3-33.

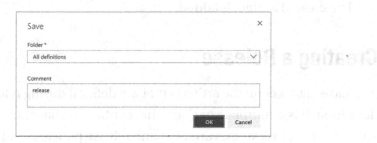

Figure 3-33. *The Save dialog box*

The release definition is created.

Adding Artifacts

An artifact is the actual deployable component of an application. In VSTS, the artifacts produced by artifact sources (or stored in artifact repositories) can be deployed. We need to link the correct artifact sources to the release definition at the time of creating a release definition. Perform the following steps to add artifacts:

1. Click the Add button in the Artifacts section. The Add Artifact dialog box appears.

2. Select the source type under the Source Type section.

3. Select the desired project type from the Project drop-down list.

4. Select the build definition that was created earlier from the Source (Build Definition) drop-down list.

5. Select the default version from the Default version drop-down list.

6. Click the Close icon to close the dialog box.

The created artifact is added.

Creating a Release

A release manages all the artifacts that are defined during release definition. It is a complete package that contains a snapshot of environments, task steps, variables, and release policies used to perform all operations in the release definition. Perform the following steps to create a release:

1. Click the Release button. A drop-down list appears.

2. Click the Create Release option. The Create New Release dialog box appears.

3. Select the environment from the Environments for Trigger Change from Automated to Manual drop-down list.

4. Enter the desired release description in the Description text box.

5. Click the Create button, as shown in Figure 3-34.

Figure 3-34. *The Create New Release dialog box*

A release is created.

Deploying a Release

Once the release is created successfully, we can deploy it to the resource group created on Azure. Perform the following steps to deploy the release:

1. Select the Release tab. The created release is shown.

2. Click the ellipsis ••• icon. A context menu appears.

3. Select the Open option from the context menu. The Summary page of the selected release appears.

4. Click the Deploy button. A drop-down list appears.

5. Select the desired option from the drop-down list.
    The Deploy Release to Environment dialog box
    appears.

6. Click the Deploy button to deploy the release.

The release is deployed successfully, as shown in Figure 3-35.

Figure 3-35. *Deploying a release*

Viewing the Deployed Release

Once the release is deployed to Azure, we can view it in a web browser.
Perform the following steps to view the release:

1. Open the Azure portal.

2. Click the Resource Groups option in the left pane.
    A list of resource groups appears in the right pane.

3. Click the resource group that we linked to the
    environment. The selected resource group opens
    with the described settings.

4. Click the item that we created in the resource group.
    In this case, we created an app service. The selected
    app service opens.

5. Click the Browse button to view the service in the
    web browser.

A web browser window opens with the deployment result, as shown in
Figure 3-36.

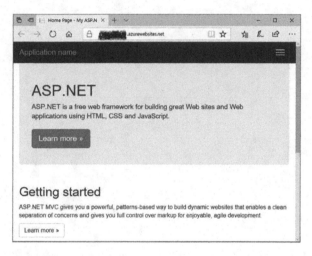

Figure 3-36. *Window showing the deployed release*

Summary

VSTS is a comprehensive CI-CD solution, which means that it manages
the entire software development lifecycle. Its support of different source
control systems, work items, and Agile methods makes it a perfect choice
for organizations. The functionality of automating the build, test, and
release processes speeds up the software release process. VSTS is a cloud-
based environment, which makes it available 24 hours a day, seven days a
week without the overhead of managing the DevOps software deployment.

CHAPTER 4

Azure Application Deployment

In the preceding chapters, we discussed DevOps fundamentals and the use of best-of-breed stand-alone DevOps Software, and we reviewed the integrated DevOps platform. The next logical step is to put it all together and manage the software development lifecycle of an Azure application. Of course, you can further enhance this solution to suit your website or enterprise software. The key here is DevOps.

This chapter discusses a real Azure application deployment using VSTS. We have a virtual machine on Azure that has e-commerce software (Magento) installed on it. We will use VSTS to deploy changes to the code automatically and view the effects on the Azure application. The solution also includes a GitHub repository to store and version source code and a shell script for installing the Azure virtual machine and Magento application.

We make changes in the VSTS Git repository, committed changes, and deployed the release. The release is then deployed to view the changes. In this scenario, we make changes to the HTML/CSS files of the source code to change the color of the menus from blue to orange and deploy a release. Figure 4-1 depicts an overview of this scenario.

© Suren Machiraju, Suraj Gaurav 2018
S. Machiraju and S. Gaurav, *DevOps for Azure Applications*,
https://doi.org/10.1007/978-1-4842-3643-7_4

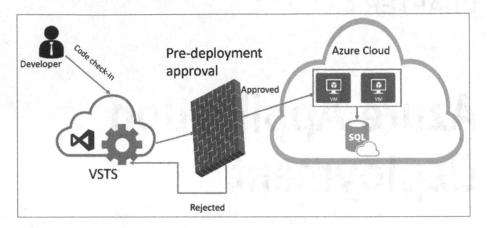

Figure 4-1. *Scenario overview*

Understanding Magento

Magento is an open source e-commerce platform. It allows developers to easily create a shopping cart for their online stores. It also allows developers to have better control over the content, appearance, and functionality of their online stores. It provides features such as search engine optimization and support for catalog-management tools.

Magento is extremely simple to use and can be used by individuals who are not experienced developers. The availability of a number of themes and plug-ins makes it effective in enhancing the customers' experience. Considerable support is available through its large volunteer community.

Benefits of Using Magento

There are several benefits of using Magento. Some of them are as follows:

- Easy installation.

- Provides several layouts and plug-ins that can be used to add more functionality to the e-commerce solution.

- Supports many payment gateways.

- It is an open source technology, which means that it can be modified based on user requirements.

Disadvantages of Magento

The following disadvantages/limitations are associated with Magento:

- A more complex system compared to Drupal.

- Requires complex programming to add custom functionality.

- Requires experienced developers to enable it to integrate with other systems.

Prerequisites of Running an Azure Application with Magento

There are a few prerequisites needed to run an Azure application with Magento. A system must have:

- A virtual machine on Azure running Linux

- Apache server

- MySQL

- PHP

Setting Up Magento

In this scenario, we used an ARM template to set up Magento. This template contains the source code and shell scripts for setting up a virtual machine on Azure and installing all the prerequisites and Magento on the created virtual machine. This template also contains a file that creates a button. Users utilize that button to navigate to Azure in order to deploy the virtual machine and launch the Magento application.

Note   To use Azure cloud, you need an Azure subscription.

Perform the following steps to set up Magento:

1. Click the Deploy to Azure button to deploy a Magento package, as shown in Figure 4-2.

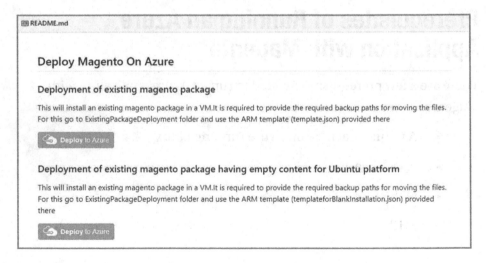

Figure 4-2. Deploying Magento

After clicking the Deploy to Azure button, you are redirected to the Azure login page, wherein you need to specify an email and password to log in. Once the authorization is done, the Custom Deployment page appears.

2. Select the subscription details from the Subscription drop-down list.

3. Select the desired radio button beside the Resource Group option to specify whether to create a new resource group or use an existing resource group. In this case, we selected the Create New radio button.

4. Specify the name of the resource group in the Create a Resource Group text box.

5. Select the desired location from the Location drop-down list.

6. Specify a domain name in the Domain Name text box.

7. Specify the name of the customer in the Customer ID text box.

8. Specify the tier of customer subscription in the Customer Tier text box.

9. Specify the password for MySQL in the My SQL Password text box.

10. Specify the username of the virtual machine server admin in the VM Admin Username text box.

11. Specify the password of the virtual machine server admin in the VM Admin Password text box.

The values for fields—including Magento File Backup (backup of Magento files), Magento Media Backup (backup of media files), Magento Init Backup (backup of INIT folder content), Magento Var Backup (backup of VAR folder content), Magento Default HTaccess (default htaccess file), Magento DB Backup (backup of Magento DB), and virtual machine size (size of the required virtual machine)—are automatically completed through the ARM template.

12. Click the Purchase button, as shown in Figure 4-3.

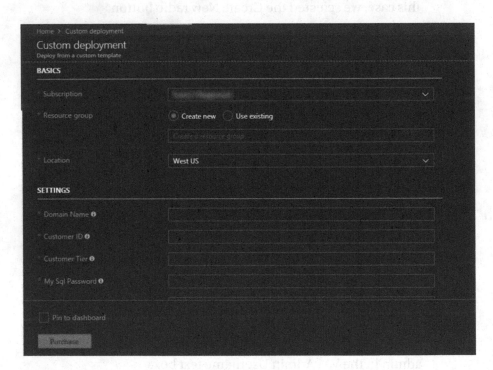

Figure 4-3. *The Custom Deployment page*

It takes a few minutes after clicking the Purchase button to get a successful deployment. Once the deployment is successful, the virtual machine starts running. We can view the artifacts by visiting the created resource group, as shown in Figure 4-4.

Figure 4-4. *Viewing artifacts*

To view the deployment history, click the deployment under the Deployment History section of the created resource group. Here, we will get the URL under the INSTALLEDURL text box under the Outputs section. If we run this URL in any web browser, we get the Magento website, as shown in Figure 4-5.

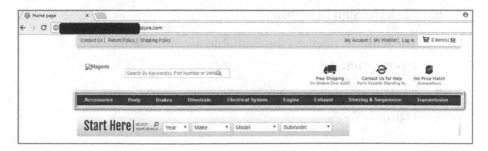

Figure 4-5. *The Magento website*

Source Code Integration with Git

A source code repository is a file archive location where source code for software is placed so that it can be accessed when required. It can be stored publicly or privately. The source code repository is used to handle several versions of a project.

VSTS supports two types of source code repositories, as follows:

- TFS-based repositories

- Git-based repositories

In this section, we are going to create a Git-based repository to store the source code.

Creating a Repository in VSTS

Perform the following steps to create a Git-based repository in VSTS:

1. Navigate to `https://www.visualstudio.com/`.

2. Click the Sign In button. The Sign In page appears.

3. Enter the email address in the Email or Phone text box.

4. Click the Next button.

5. Enter the password in the Password text box.

6. Click the Sign In button.

    The window displays the available accounts and repositories.

7. Click the Create New Account button, as shown in Figure 4-6.

Figure 4-6. *Creating a new account*

When you click the Create New Account button, a
new window appears where you need to enter the
account-related details.

8. Enter the name of the subdomain in the Host My
    Projects At text box.

9. Select the Git radio button to manage code
    using Git.

10. Enter the name of the project in the Project Name
    text box.

11. Select the framework from the Organize Work Using
    the drop-down list.

12. Select the hosting location from the Host Your
    Projects In The drop-down list.

13. Click the Continue button, as shown in Figure 4-7.

Figure 4-7. *Hosting the project*

The project-creation process starts. Once the process completes, the project is created.

If you already have a VSTS account, you can create a repository by performing the following steps:

1. Open the VSTS account.

2. Click the New Team Project option, as shown in Figure 4-8.

Figure 4-8. *Clicking the New Team Project option*

The Create New Project page appears.

3. Enter the desired name of the project in the Project Name text box.

4. Enter the desired description in the Description text box.

5. Select the Git option from the Version Control drop-down list to create a Git repository.

6. Select the Agile option from the Work Item Process drop-down list.

7. Click the Create button, as shown in Figure 4-9.

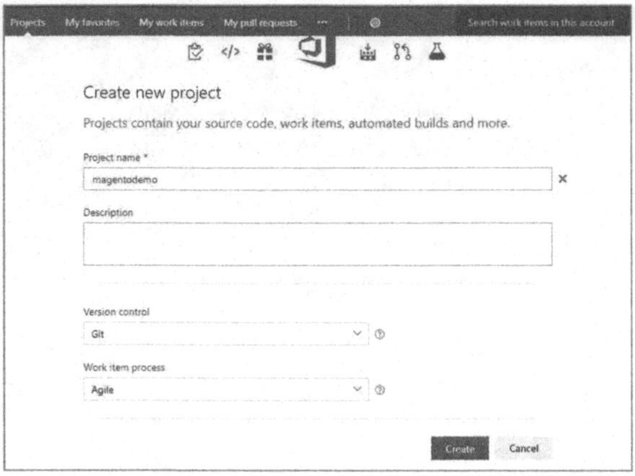

Figure 4-9. *Creating a project*

The project is created successfully.

Uploading Code on VSTS Git

Once the repository is created successfully, we need to upload or add code to the repository. We used Visual Studio IDE to upload the source code.

Perform the following steps to upload a code file to the VSTS Git-based repository:

1. Hover the mouse over the Code button. A list of options appears.

2. Select the repository we created earlier, as shown in Figure 4-10.

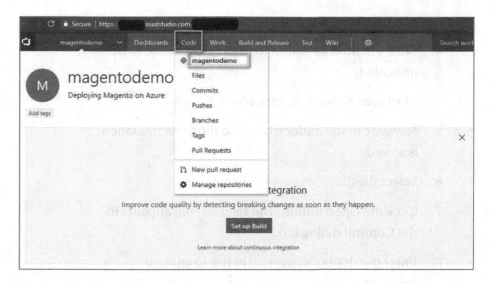

Figure 4-10. *Selecting the repository*

The files associated with the selected repository appear.

3. Click the Upload File(s) button to upload a new file, as shown in Figure 4-11.

Figure 4-11. *Clicking the Upload File(s) button*

The Commit dialog box appears.

4. Click the Browse button to search for the file to be uploaded.

The Open dialog box appears.

5. Navigate to the folder where the file to be uploaded is stored.

6. Select the file.

7. Click the Open button. The selected file appears in the Commit dialog box.

8. Enter the desired comment in the Comment text area.

9. Click the Commit button to commit the changes, as shown in Figure 4-12.

Figure 4-12. *Uploading a file*

Creating a Release Definition

Once the file is uploaded to the repository, we need to create a release definition in VSTS. A release definition describes the application's overall release process. This application must be deployed in different environments.

Perform the following steps to create a release definition in VSTS:

1. Navigate to the project we created earlier.

2. Hover the mouse over the Build and Release button. A list of options appears.

3. Click the Releases option, as shown in Figure 4-13.

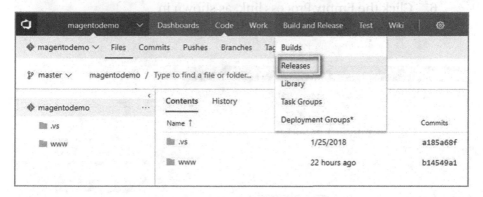

Figure 4-13. *Clicking the Releases option*

4. Click the + button. A drop-down list appears.

5. Click the Create Release Definition option, as shown in Figure 4-14.

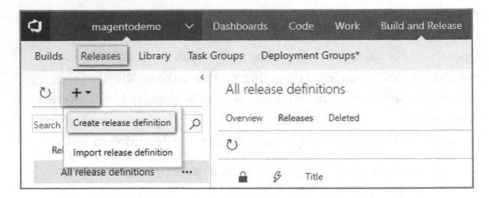

Figure 4-14. *Click the Create Release Definition option*

The Select a Template dialog box appears.

6. Click the Empty Process link, as shown in
    Figure 4-15.

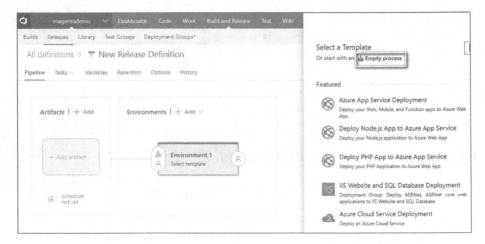

Figure 4-15. *The Select a Template dialog box*

7. Click the Add Artifact button under the Artifacts section.

    The Add Artifact dialog box appears.

8. Select the Git option under the Source Type section.

9. Select the desired project from the Project drop-down list.

10. Select the desired Source repository from the Source (Repository) drop-down list.

11. Select the default branch from the Default Branch drop-down list.

12. Select the default version from the Default Version drop-down list, as shown in Figure 4-16.

Figure 4-16. *Selecting the source type*

13.   Specify the desired source alias in the Source Alias text box.

14.   Click the Add button, as shown in Figure 4-17.

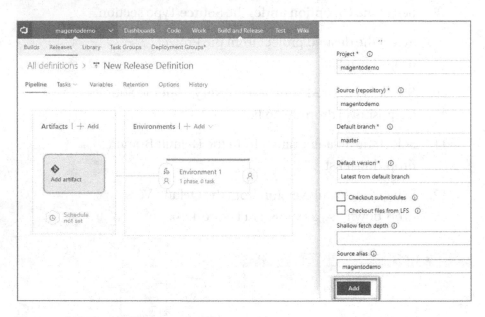

Figure 4-17. *Adding an artifact*

The created artifact is added.

15.   Edit the release definition name, as shown in Figure 4-18.

Figure 4-18. *Editing the release definition name*

16. Click the Environment 1 button under the Environments section. The Environment dialog box appears.

17. Replace the Environment 1 text in the Environment Name text box with the desired text to specify a unique name for the environment.

18. Click the Close button to close the Environment dialog box.

19. Select the Tasks tab. A list of related tasks appears in the left pane, and the description of the selected task appears in the right pane, as shown in Figure 4-19.

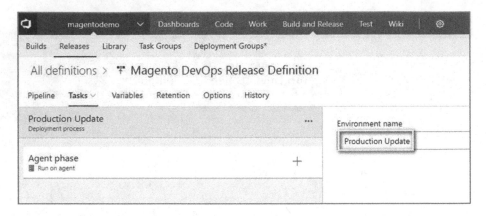

Figure 4-19. *Selecting the Tasks tab*

> 20.   Select the Agent Phase option in the left pane. Many
>   options related to the selection appear in the right
>   pane, as shown in Figure 4-20.

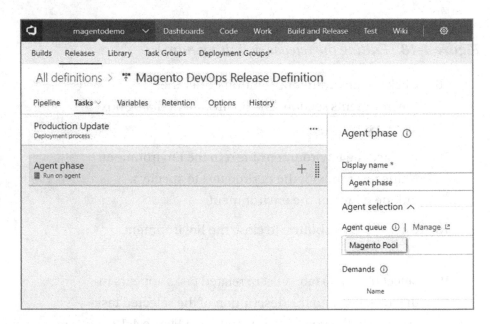

Figure 4-20. *Options related to the agent phase*

In Figure 4-20, the agent appearing in the Agent
Queue text box is deployed by the ARM template.

Note   A phase groups the tasks created under it. It defines the
runtime target environment to execute the created tasks. On an
agent, the tasks are executed by an agent phase in a queue.

---

21. Click the + icon beside the Agent Phase option to
     add a new task to the agent. The Add Tasks pane
     appears on the right side with a list of available
     tasks.

22. Select the Shell Script option from the list to add a
     shell script task. The Add button becomes active.

23. Click the Add button to add the selected task, as
     shown in Figure 4-21.

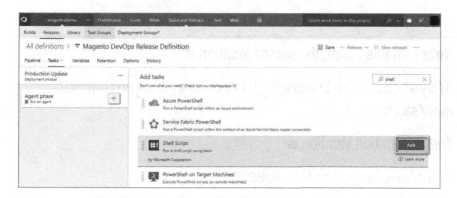

Figure 4-21. *Adding a task*

The selected task is added to the agent.

24.   Select the added task in the left pane. The settings associated with the selected task appear in the right pane.

25.   Select the desired version of the selected shell script from the Version drop-down list.

26.   Specify the desired display name for the selected task in the Display Name text box.

27.   Select the Inline radio button under the Type section to add an inline script.

28.   Add the following inline script to remotely copy files from a source location to the destination location in the Script text area:

```
sudo rsync -ar "$(System.DefaultWorkingDirectory)/magentodemo/
www/skin" /var/www/magento/2016080806
```

Note   In this script, the source location is:

```
$(System.DefaultWorkingDirectory)/magentodemo/
www/skin
```

The destination location is:

```
/var/www/magento/2016080806
```

---

29.   Click the Save button to save the release definition, as shown in Figure 4-22.

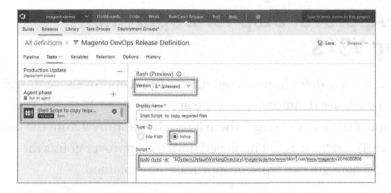

Figure 4-22. *Adding a script to the task*

As we click the Save button, the Save dialog box appears.

30. Select the desired folder from the Folder drop-down list.

31. Enter the desired comment in the Comment text box.

32. Click the OK button, as shown in Figure 4-23.

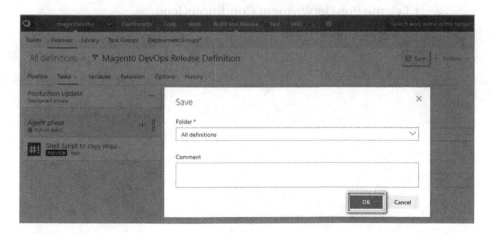

Figure 4-23. *Saving the release definition*

Pre-Approval Step for Deployment Using VSTS

Once the release definition is created, we can set approvals for the release within the release definition. Once the approvals have been set, the deployment stops at the stage where it requires approval from the assigned approver. The release is not deployed until the approver grants the approval. There are two types of approvals, as explained:

- **Pre-approval:** This type of approval is required before starting the deployment process.

- **Post-approval:** This type of approval is required once the deployment is complete. It is used when deploying to multiple environments like Test, Staging, and Production.

Perform the following steps to add the pre-approval step for deployment:

1. Open the release definition.

2. Click the Pre-Deployment Conditions icon, as shown in Figure 4-24.

Figure 4-24. *Clicking the Pre-Deployment Conditions icon*

The Pre-Deployment Conditions dialog box appears.

3. Enable the Pre-Deployment Approvals option.

4. Locate and select the desired approver from the Approvers search box.

Note   We can add single or multiple approvers both for pre-deployment and post-deployment settings. An approver can be an individual user or a group of users. When a group is set as an approver, the deployment can be approved by only one of the users in the group.

---

5. Specify the timeout settings for the approval in the
    Timeout section. If the approval is not approved within
    the specified timeout period, the deployment is rejected.

6. Select the desired checkbox under the Approval
    Policies section. The following checkboxes are
    available under the Approval Policies section:

    - **The user requesting a release or deployment
      should not approve:** When this checkbox is selected,
      the user who is requesting (initiated or created) the
      release cannot approve it. To approve or reject our
      own deployments, this checkbox needs to be cleared.

    - **Skip approval if the same approver approved the
      previous environment:** This policy states that the
      approval is skipped if the previous environment is
      approved by the same approver set for the current
      environment. If there are multiple approvers, the
      approval becomes pending for them.

7. Click the Save button, as shown in Figure 4-25.

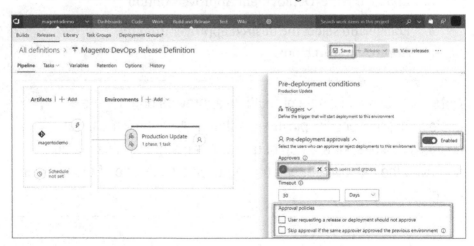

Figure 4-25. *Pre-deployment conditions dialog box*

The pre-approval deployment has been configured, as shown in Figure 4-26.

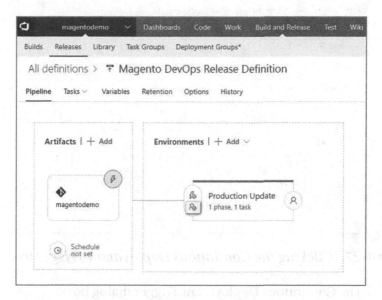

Figure 4-26. *Successful pre-approval deployment*

Automated Continuous Deployments Using VSTS

A release definition can be configured such that a new release is automatically created when new artifacts are available, or when the latest code is checked in. Such continuous deployment can be automated through VSTS.

Perform the following steps to configure continuous deployment:

1. Click the Continuous Deployment Trigger icon under the Artifacts section, as shown in Figure 4-27.

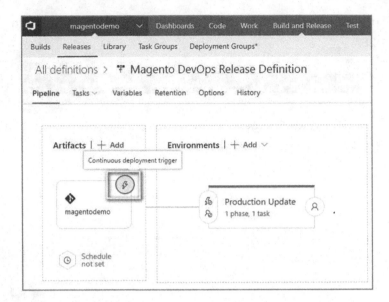

Figure 4-27. *Clicking the Continuous Deployment Trigger icon*

The Continuous Deployment Trigger dialog box appears.

2. Enable the Continuous Deployment Trigger option.

3. Click the Save button, as shown in Figure 4-28.

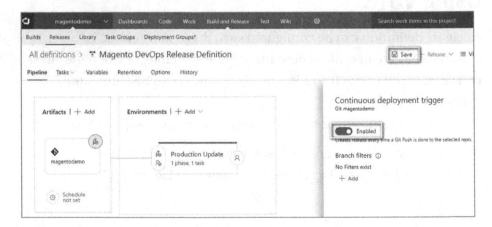

Figure 4-28. *The Continuous Deployment Trigger dialog box*

The continuous deployment trigger is enabled, as shown in Figure 4-29.

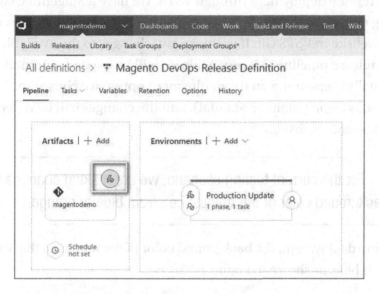

Figure 4-29. *Successful continuous deployment*

There are three options for triggering deployment, which are:

- **Manual:** This option creates a new release manually by selecting the Release icon in a release definition. This option does not create a release automatically when there is a new build of source artifacts available.

- **Continuous deployment:** This option creates a new release automatically when new build artifacts are available. This option allows us to specify the artifact sources linked to the release definition to trigger a new release.

- **Scheduled:** This option creates a new release automatically based on the specified schedule. Select the days of the week and the time of day to define a schedule for automatically creating a new release.

Testing the Deployment

We can test the deployment through VSTS. We have a Magento website running on a virtual machine on Azure portal. We have the entire code for the website in VSTS Git. If we make any changes to the available code, a release pipeline will run, a release will be created automatically or manually (depending on the deployment option we chose, i.e., Continuous Deployment or Manual), and the changes will be reflected on the Magento website.

Note   For the current testing scenario, we are making changes to the background color of the menus, i.e., from blue to orange.

Before deployment, the background color of the menus in the Magento website is blue, as shown in Figure 4-30.

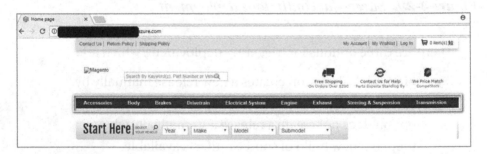

Figure 4-30. *Existing Magento website*

Testing Continuous Deployment of Release

Perform the following steps to deploy the release automatically:

1. Log in to the VSTS account.

2. Hover the mouse over the Code tab. A list of options appears.

3. Select the Files option from the list.

4. Navigate to the `styles.css` file. The content of the selected file appears in the right pane under the Contents tab selected by default.

5. Click the Edit button, as shown in Figure 4-31.

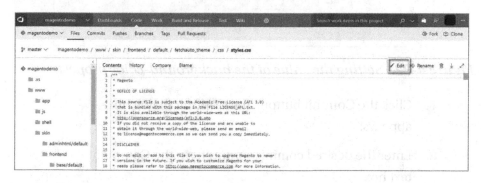

Figure 4-31. *Navigating to the style.css file*

6. Set the value of the `background-color` property under the `cssmenu` class to `orange`, as shown in Figure 4-32.

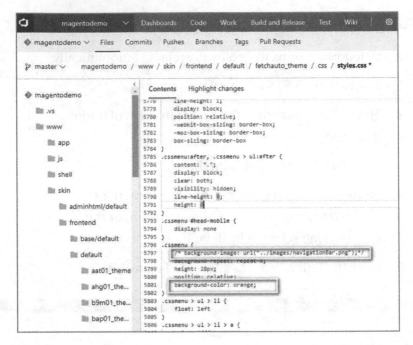

Figure 4-32. *Setting the value of the background-color property*

7. Click the Commit button. The Commit dialog box appears.

8. Enter the desired commit comment in the Comment text box.

9. Click the Commit button to commit the changes, as shown in Figure 4-33.

Figure 4-33. *Committing changes*

The code changes are committed successfully, as shown in Figure 4-34.

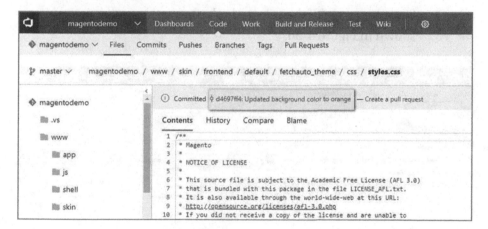

Figure 4-34. *Successful commit*

Since we have correctly configured our process for continuous deployment, the release pipeline will start once the code is committed.

10. Open the release definition created earlier. In this case, we created the release definition named Magento DevOps Release Definition. Here, we can see that a new release named Release-3 is created, as shown in Figure 4-35.

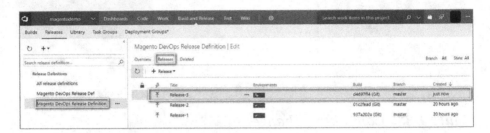

Figure 4-35. *Opening the release definition*

11. Click the Release-3 release to view its details. The Summary page of the selected release appears, as shown in Figure 4-36.

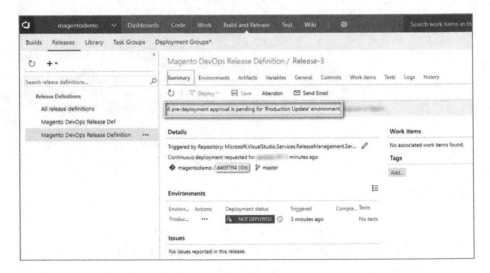

Figure 4-36. *The Summary page of the selected release*

In Figure 4-36, we can see that the deployment status under the Environments section states that the release is not deployed yet. We require a pre-deployment approval from the approver before the actual deployment of the release. In this case, the approver received an email to review the release and approve or reject it.

12.   Click the View Approval button, as shown in Figure 4-37.

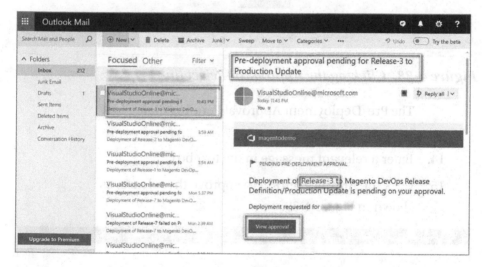

Figure 4-37. *Viewing email for approval*

The approver is redirected to the Summary page of the release created earlier.

13.   Click the Approve or Reject link, as shown in Figure 4-38.

107

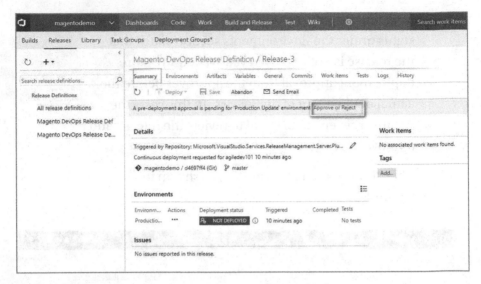

Figure 4-38. *Clicking the Approve or Reject link*

The Pre-Deployment Approval Pending dialog box appears.

14. Enter a relevant message in the text box.

15. Click the Approve button to approve the release, as shown in Figure 4-39.

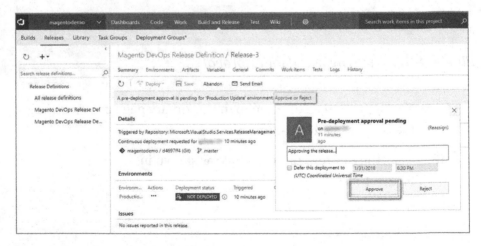

Figure 4-39. *The Pre-Deployment Approval Pending dialog box*

Once the approver clicks the Approve button,
the deployment starts. Its status can be seen
in the Deployment Status option under the
Environments section of the Summary page, as
shown in Figure 4-40.

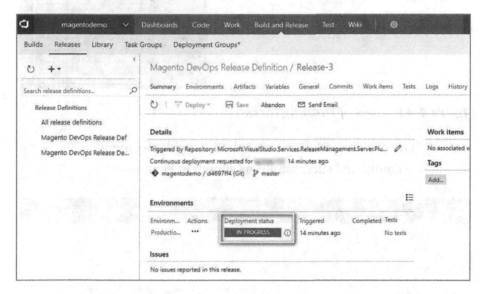

Figure 4-40. *Status of deployment*

16.   Select the Logs tab to monitor the deployment, as
      shown in Figure 4-41.

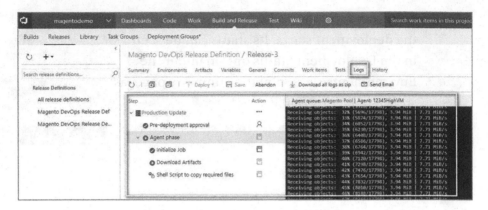

Figure 4-41. *Logs of running tasks*

Once all the tasks have completed, the deployment
is completed successfully, as shown in Figure 4-42.

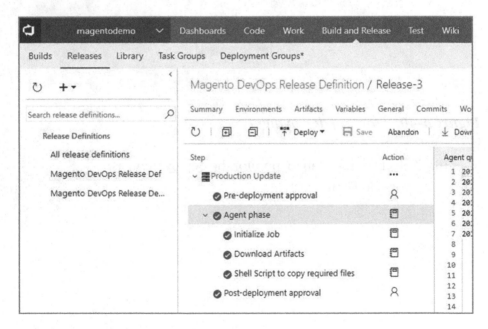

Figure 4-42. *Tasks completion status*

17. Select the Summary tab to view the summary of the
     created release.

     The Summary page displays the value of the
     Deployment Status option under the Environments
     section as SUCCEEDED, as shown in Figure 4-43.

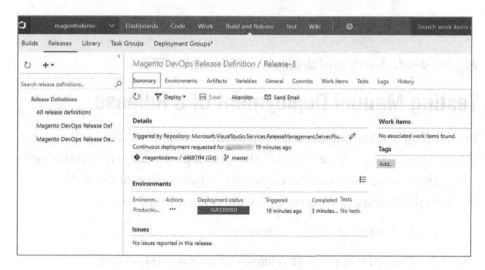

Figure 4-43. *The deployment status*

     Once the deployment is successful, we can refresh
     the home page of the Magento website. Once the
     page refreshes, we can see that the background
     color of the menus has changed from blue to
     orange, which means that the VSTS deployment was
     successful, as shown in Figure 4-44.

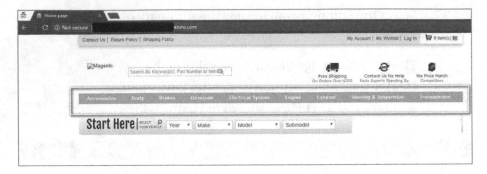

Figure 4-44. *Successful deployment through VSTS*

Testing Manual Deployment of a Release

Even though the automated release was successful, we should still test the
manual deployment in case the continuous deployment is not configured
correctly, or in case we want to deploy the older version of the code.
Perform the following steps to deploy the release manually:

1. Log in to the VSTS account.

2. Open the applicable release definition, as shown in
   Figure 4-45.

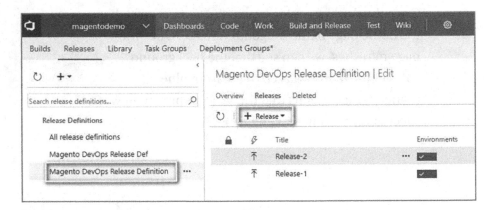

Figure 4-45. *Opening the release definition*

3. Click the Release button. A drop-down list appears.

4. Click the Create Release option, as shown in Figure 4-46.

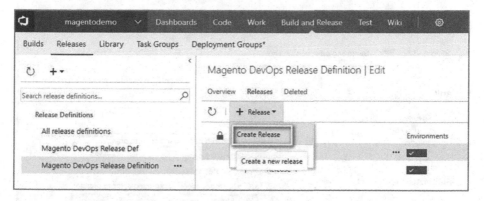

Figure 4-46. *Creating a new release*

The Create New Release for Magento DevOps Release Definition dialog box appears.

5. Enter the desired description for the release in the Release Description text box.

6. Select the b14549a1 (Updated Background Color To 'Light Blue') option from the Version drop-down list to set the background color of the menus to light blue.

7. Click the Create button to create a new release, as
    shown in Figure 4-47.

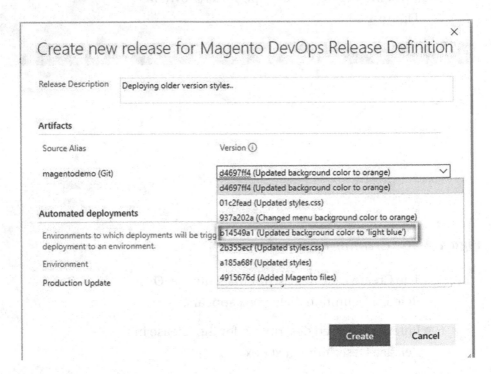

Figure 4-47. *The Create New Release for Magento DevOps Release
Definition dialog box*

The release pipeline starts, and the manual
deployment icon displays for the created release in
the Environments column, as shown in Figure 4-48.

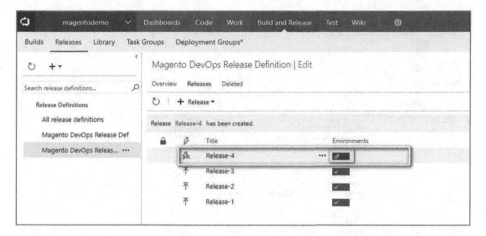

Figure 4-48. *Viewing the manual deployment icon*

The approver receives an email with a link to View Deployment, along with additional controls to approve or reject the deployment. Once the approvers click the View Deployment button, they are redirected to the release definition.

8. Click the Approve or Reject link. The Pre-Deployment Approval Pending dialog box appears.

9. Enter the desired comment in the Type Comments Here text box.

10. Click the Approve button to approve the release deployment, as shown in Figure 4-49.

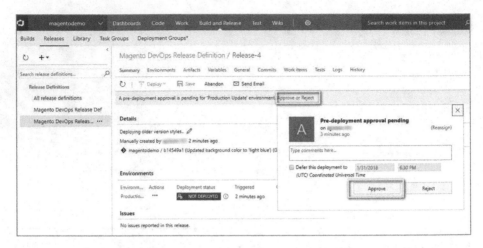

Figure 4-49. *Approving the release deployment*

Once the approver clicks the Approve button,
the deployment begins, and all tasks complete
successfully, as shown in Figure 4-50.

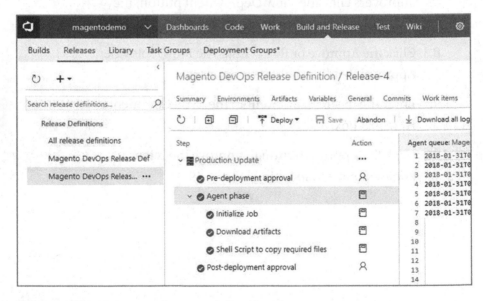

Figure 4-50. *Status of successful tasks*

11. Select the Summary tab. The Summary page appears, and we can see that the value of the Deployment Status option displays as SUCCEEDED, as shown in Figure 4-51.

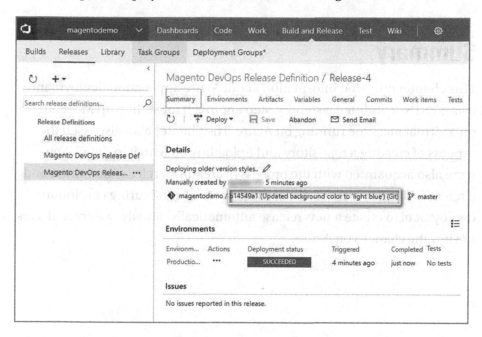

Figure 4-51. *Successful deployment*

12. Refresh the Magento website. The background color of the website will now be light blue, as shown in Figure 4-52.

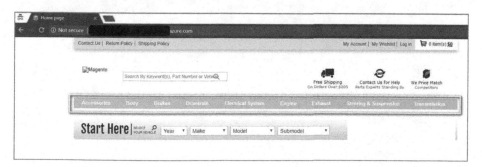

Figure 4-52. *Final output*

With this build, we have successfully used VSTS as a DevOps platform to manage the software development lifecycle from the first deployment to subsequent updates.

Summary

This chapter provided information about Azure application deployment using VSTS. It outlined a step-by-step approach for setting up Magento on a virtual machine running on Azure. The chapter also discussed the process of creating a repository and uploading code to it in detail. You were also acquainted with the process of creating a release definition and a release. You also learned about the process of configuring continuous deployment to create a new release automatically. Finally, we created a test to view the changes on Azure.

CHAPTER 5

Final Thoughts

This chapter takes a look back at the discussions from the preceding chapters.

DevOps for Azure

Chapter 1 presented basic DevOps concepts. Recall that without DevOps, the manual software deployment process is error-prone, time-consuming, and inefficient due to a lack of robust process integration and poor team communication. The manual process also slows down performance.

The DevOps solution replaces the manual process of application deployment, wherein DevOps automates the entire process of software development and deployment. DevOps integrates the functionality of both the Development and Operations/Production teams into the application deployment process. One of DevOps most important functions is its ability to automate the process of application deployment, allowing multiple developers to check in and check out code simultaneously in/from the Source repository, etc.

In the DevOps application deployment process, developers write code and check it into the source control/Source repository. The Continuous Integration (CI) server generates the build. During the build process, several tasks are performed, including automated unit testing, code

© Suren Machiraju, Suraj Gaurav 2018
S. Machiraju and S. Gaurav, *DevOps for Azure Applications*,
https://doi.org/10.1007/978-1-4842-3643-7_5

coverage, and code analysis. If there is an error, a report is automatically generated and sent back to the developer for correction in the code. Then, a release is created for the successful build in which testing, QA, and staging operations begin. Once a successful release is available, the release is deployed to the target environment—Microsoft Azure Cloud. The first chapter also introduced a number of different DevOps tools.

Deployment via TeamCity and Octopus Deploy

Chapter 2 outlined how to deploy a package on Azure Web Application using best-of-breed tools—a Continuous Integration (CI) tool (TeamCity) and a Continuous Delivery (CD) tool (Octopus Deploy). TeamCity is a Continuous Integration server for developers powered by JetBrains.

Using TeamCity, we demonstrated how to create a project and specify the build configuration by providing the SVN (subversion) path to include the latest code and placing it in the build agent. Our process created a successful build in TeamCity. Afterward, we configured the source code and set parameters for the PowerShell script file. The target path settings were modified to create a NuGet package. This package was placed at a location accessible by Octopus Deploy.

Octopus Deploy is an automated deployment server that streamlines and automates the deployment process of different applications into different environments. This process thus becomes practically effortless. Using Octopus Deploy, we created a project. Then, we created two environments and we uploaded the package. We also created two steps within that package, and we created a release for the project. Last, we deployed the release, and the deployment resulted in the successful deployment of the content of the NuGet package on the Azure websites.

Deployment via VSTS

Chapter 3 discussed deploying a web application using a completely integrated DevOps platform called Visual Studio Team Services (VSTS).

VSTS is a collaborative CI-CD solution. This means that VSTS manages the entire software development lifecycle, from creating packages to deploying applications. It is a cloud-based environment, which means it's available 24 hours a day, seven days a week without any management or operations overhead.

Using VSTS, we first created an account to host the project, and we created a project under the account. We then added the source code to the project and made a few changes to the source code. We then committed the changes and created a build. Once the build was successful, a release definition was created. The release definition describes an application's end-to-end release process so that it can be deployed to different environments. After creating the release definition, we added artifacts and environments to which the application could be deployed. Then, a release was created. A release is a complete package that contains a snapshot of environments, task steps, variables, and release policies that are used to perform all the operations in the release definition. After creating the release, we deployed it to the resource group created on Azure. The release was deployed successfully on Azure.

Azure Application Deployment

Chapter 4 applied what we covered in previous chapters to an Azure application deployment using VSTS. We created a virtual machine on Azure and installed an e-commerce application called Magento. We committed changes to the source code through VSTS and deployed the changes on the Magento application running on Azure. A release was created and deployed to view the effects of the changes made to the source code.

Now that you have completed the step-by-step process, with additional details provided about the process and tools available, you are well versed and fully trained to utilize both Continuous Deployment and manual deployment methods.

Index

© Suren Machiraju, Suraj Gaurav 2018
S. Machiraju and S. Gaurav, *DevOps for Azure Applications*,
https://doi.org/10.1007/978-1-4842-3643-7

D, E, F, G, H, I, J, K, L

M

W, X, Y, Z

Printed in the United States
By Bookmasters